THE SECRET OF THE BIRD'S SMART BRAIN ... AND MORE!

BY ANA MARÍA RODRÍGUEZ

ANIMAL
SECRETS
REVEALED!

T0017357

Enslow Publishing
101 W. 23rd Street
Suite 240
New York, NY 10011
USA
enslow.com

Acknowledgments
The author expresses her immense gratitude to all the scientists who have contributed to the Animal Secrets Revealed! series. Their comments and photos have been invaluable to the creation of these books.

Published in 2018 by Enslow Publishing, LLC.
101 W. 23rd Street, Suite 240, New York, NY 10011

Copyright © 2018 by Enslow Publishing, LLC.

All rights reserved.

No part of this book may be reproduced by any means without the written permission of the publisher.

Library of Congress Cataloging-in-Publication Data

Names: Rodriguez, Ana Maria, 1958- author.
Title: The secret of the bird's smart brain... and more! / Ana María Rodríguez.
Description: New York : Enslow Publishing, 2018. | Series: Animal secrets revealed! | Includes bibliographical references and index. | Audience: Grades 3 to 6.
Identifiers: LCCN 2017002991| ISBN 9780766086234 (library-bound) | ISBN 9780766088528 (pbk.) | ISBN 9780766088467 (6-pack)
Subjects: LCSH: Birds—Juvenile literature. | Mammals—Behavior—Juvenile literature. | Animal behavior—Research—Juvenile literature.
Classification: LCC QL676.2 .R636 2017 | DDC 598.15—dc23
LC record available at https://lccn.loc.gov/2017002991

Printed in the United States of America

To Our Readers: We have done our best to make sure all websites in this book were active and appropriate when we went to press. However, the author and the publisher have no control over and assume no liability for the material available on those websites or on any websites they may link to. Any comments or suggestions can be sent by email to customerservice@enslow.com.

Photo Credits: Cover Eric Isselee/Shutterstock.com; pp. 3 (top left), 7 (top) © Eric Gevaert/Dreamstime.com; pp. 3 (top right), 13 (top) Nicole Gerlach; pp. 3 (bottom right), 28, 30, 31, 32 Marianne Wondrak, Messerli Research Institute; pp. 3 (bottom left), 35, 36 Jim Darlington; pp. 3 (center left), 21 © roblan/Dreamstime.com; p. 7 (bottom) © Gsrethees/Dreamstime.com; p. 8 © Photopitu/Dreamstime.com; p. 10 Pavel Němec; p. 11 (left) © Stephenmeese/Dreamstime.com; p. 11 (right) © Iouri Timofeev/Dreamstime.com; pp. 13 (bottom), 42 Ana María S. Rodríguez; p. 15 Danielle Whittaker; p. 18 Jamie Tanner; p. 23 © Erikmandre/Dreamstime.com; p. 25 Scandinavian Brown Bear Project; pp. 29, 33 Ariane Veit, Messerli Research Institute; p. 37 Seth Burdick; p. 39 Judith Janisch; p. 40 Stephan Reber.

★ CONTENTS ★

★

ENTER THE WORLD OF ANIMAL SECRETS

In this volume of Animal Secrets Revealed!, you will first take a close look at the brains of birds and discover what makes some birds very smart. Next, you will take a trip to Mountain Lake, Virginia, where birds called juncos reveal a secret about their "perfume." Then, you will travel to Swedish forests where mama bears use a curious strategy to protect their cubs. Next, you will take a trip to Vienna, Austria, and meet the scientists who uncovered a message in pig grunts. Finally, you will visit with the Swiss scientist who listens to alligator bellows.

Welcome to the world of animal secrets!

1
THE SECRET OF THE SMART BIRD'S BRAIN

A package of tiny brains is in the mail. Brain scientist Pavel Němec is excited about studying them in his lab. The brains are tiny. They are from small mammals that live in South Africa. The smallest brains weigh as much as half of an M&M® candy (about 0.02 ounces or 0.5 grams). The largest are as heavy as a shelled peanut (close to 0.1 ounces or 2.5 grams).

The brains are traveling from South Africa to Prague in the Czech Republic, where Němec runs his lab at Charles University. It's a long trip: 8,750 miles (14,082 kilometers)—about three times the distance across the United States. Nevertheless, Němec is not expecting any major problems with the delivery. He has completed the paperwork to allow the brains to travel smoothly through the customs department, where they will enter the Czech Republic.[1]

But the phone rings, and a customs' official begins questioning Němec about this package of brains from South Africa. He was suspicious. Brains, he thought, are not supposed to be so small. Are these real brains? Yes, Němec confirmed. These are tiny brains from small animals. The customs official had not thought that brains could be so small. Once convinced, he delivered the brains to Němec.

Birds Are Smart

Němec is comparing the small brains from South African mammals to the brains of birds. He is curious because birds are intelligent like mammals, yet their brains are much smaller.

"Most people think that birds are not smart," said Němec. "Scientists, however, have known for quite some time that birds are very clever."[2]

Ravens and parrots, scientists think, are among the smartest animals. They are as smart as some mammals, including chimpanzees, orangutans, and gorillas. Dolphins and dogs are also members of the "smart animal club." Like smart mammals, ravens and parrots can make and use tools, plan for future needs, and learn from their own experiences. They can even recognize themselves in a mirror. Parrots can also learn to use words or symbols to communicate with people. They can do all this with brains that are smaller than those of smart mammals.

Macaws communicate with each other.

California crows have been observed shaping thin pieces of wire into hooks to "fish" worms from holes in the ground. They also sharpen forked or single twigs against rocks and use them to spear small meals.

Crows are smart enough to use twigs and wire to get food.

Ravens have been observed retrieving food that is floating inside a vertical, transparent tube. The food is too low in the tube for the bird to grab with its beak. In order to get the food, the raven raises the level of water by adding pebbles to the tube. The raven adds pebbles until the food floats high enough for it to catch it with its beak. Many young children cannot figure this one out!

A common raven looks similar to a crow, and it is a smart bird, too.

A famous parrot named Alex worked with scientists for thirty years. Both Alex and the scientists learned something from this relationship: Alex learned a number of symbols with which he could communicate, and the scientists learned that humans and birds have more in common than they had initially thought.

Different Brains, But Both Are Smart

Once scientists realized that parrots and ravens do many of the same things as smart mammals, the scientists became interested in looking into the brains of birds. Think of your brain as a computer—one that allows you to smell food, hear music, and recognize friends. Humans use this computer to learn how to kick a soccer ball, tie shoelaces, and play a musical instrument. Without this living computer in our heads, we could not express emotions like happiness or sadness. We could not plan a camping trip or develop a strategy to win a video game.

Because ravens and parrots are as smart as smart mammals, scientists expected that their brains would look very similar. They were surprised to see that the brains of birds and mammals have important differences.[4]

The forebrain is the part of the brain that allows smart mammals and birds to make tools or plan ahead. In mammals, the forebrain is made of layers

> **Science Tongue Twisters:**
> **Here are the scientific names of some of the birds studied in this project:**
> Raven, *Corvus corax*; Sulfur-crested cockatoo, *Cacatua galerita*; Blue and yellow macaw, *Ara ararauna*; Barn owl, *Tyto alba*; Starling, *Stumus vulgaris*

of brain cells or neurons. In birds, however, neurons in the forebrain are not in layers, but instead form clusters. There is more than one way for the brain to be smart.

Still, scientists had not answered the big question: How can a small brain make a bird smart? Němec and his colleagues decided to look at bird brains even closer. They decided to count the number of cells in bird brains and compare them with the numbers of cells in mammal brains.

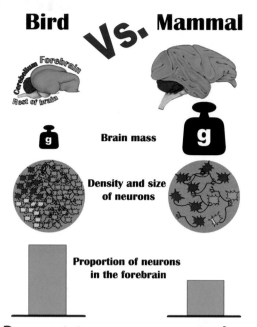

Bird vs. Mammal

Brain mass

Density and size
of neurons

Proportion of neurons
in the forebrain

By containing more neurons in the same area, some bird brains help the birds be smarter!

Counting Brain Cells

Seweryn Olkowicz and Martin Kocourek, students in Němec's lab, took on the project. They collected the brains of seventy-three individual birds from twenty-eight different species and counted the number of brain cells using a technique called the isotropic fractionator. The technique allowed them to count individual cells very quickly. Then they compared those numbers with those from mammal brains of the same weight.[5]

Olkowicz and Kocourek discovered that the brains of birds such as parrots and songbirds have twice as many neurons as monkey brains of the same weight. Olkowicz, Kocourek, Němec, and their colleagues discovered the secret of the smart bird's brain—a gram (or ounce) of a smart bird's brain tightly packs twice the brainpower of mammal brains. Smart birds have a powerful miniature super computer in their small heads.[6]

RAVEN vs. CROW[3] Ravens and crows may look the same at first, but you can tell them apart by carefully noticing their differences.		
Feature	Raven	Crow
Size	Larger	Smaller
Tail, when open	Wedge-shaped (middle feathers are longer)	Fan-shaped (feathers are of the same length)
Sounds	Cawing sound ("caw-caw")	Lower croaking sound ("gronk-gronk")

Barn owls are one of the smartest night birds.

Starlings and other songbirds are among the smartest birds.

2

THE SECRET OF THE JUNCO'S PERFUME

A cell phone chimes a tune. It's 5 a.m. Danielle Whittaker, bird biologist, swipes her finger over the phone screen and gets ready for a day of fieldwork. "I am definitely not a morning person," she said. "But I have to get up early because the birds do."[1]

Whittaker is at Mountain Lake Biological Station in Virginia. From spring to fall, she lives in the world of the dark-eyed junco. The junco, a brown, fit-in-one-hand songbird, makes the wooded areas of North America its home. Juncos are helping Whittaker uncover a little-known characteristic about birds. Do birds use the sense of smell to communicate with other birds?

Mouse biologists, for example, have detailed answers to this question. For mice, and many other mammals, their keen sense of smell is a major gateway to the outside world. Scent helps mice find food, track other mice, and figure out which ones are females

Danielle Whittaker holds one of the juncos she captured in the forest.

and which are males. Sense of smell can help a mouse choose a partner with which to start a family.

On the other hand, male birds sing, dance, parade colorful feathers, or all of the above in an attempt to attract partners. Think of the elegant green- and blue-feathered fan of the peacock's tail, the step dance of the blue-footed

The blue-footed booby of the Galápagos Islands displays its colorful feet when it step dances to attract a female.

booby, or musical bird songs. But scent? Do birds have any use for scent when choosing mates?

Can Birds Smell?

Before she studied juncos, Whittaker studied how the gibbon, a primate found in Indonesia, selects a mate. When she returned to the United States, Whittaker continued studying how animals choose a mate, but looked at a different animal that was easier to study at home.

"I like studying birds because you can find them almost anywhere," Whittaker said.

One day, as Whittaker discussed the results of her experiments with one of her college professors, he said, "The clues you are looking for are detected by smell. But birds do not have a sense of smell. So, why would you study it?"

Whittaker was stunned.

"I had not heard that before," Whittaker said, "but the idea that this one group of animals would have no sense of smell made no sense to me."

Scientists think that smell is one of the oldest senses. It's been present in the animal kingdom since

> **Science Tongue Twister:**
> **The junco's scientific name is**
> *Junco hyemalis.*

the first animals appeared. Whittaker turned to research to find out whether birds have a sense of smell. She went to the library to study what others had written on the subject, but she could not find any answers. She also did her own experiments. Finally, she confirmed her original suspicion: the professor's statement that birds do not have a sense of smell is a myth.[2]

Since those first experiments, Whittaker and other scientists have discovered that birds can smell different kinds of odors. Birds can also produce their own scents. "It's like they wear their own perfume," said Whittaker.

The Secret Is in the Preen Gland

Juncos and other birds have a gland, called the preen gland, that produces a scented oil. The preen gland is located above

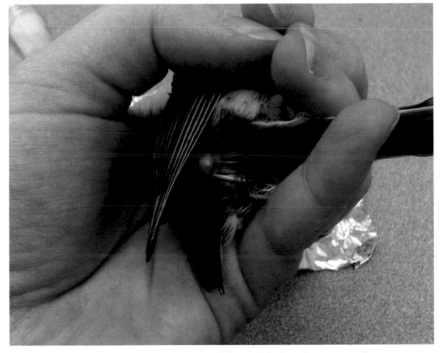

A researcher carefully holds a junco while showing the preen gland, the small bump at the base of the tail.

WATCH FOR BEARS!

If you think that trapping birds with nets in the wild might not be very exciting, just ask Whittaker about the time a bear broke into the aviary. "We had left a few birds outside in the aviary for the night and went back to the lab. The aviary is a simple enclosure we made with mesh to keep the birds temporarily before we take them back to the lab. One night, one of my colleagues had gone out for a run. When she reached the aviary she saw a pair of bright eyes. She thought it was one of us, but it turned out it was a black bear! It had ripped off the mesh to eat the birdseed. The birds had escaped, unharmed. My colleague was scared. She slowly retreated away from the aviary and then ran back to the lab as fast as she could with the news. Actually, the next day we ended up re-catching the birds that had gotten away."[13]

the base of the tail. The birds rub their beaks against the gland to remove the oil and then spread it over their feathers, a process called preening. Preen oil protects the feathers; it makes them waterproof, protects them against harmful microbes, and helps keep the bird warm. It turns out that preen oil also works as the bird's perfume.[3]

To study the oil, Whittaker takes samples from juncos' preen glands. That's why she wakes up very early in the morning—to catch juncos.

"I go into the field, open up the net, and put out bird seed to get the birds to come," said Whittaker. "My colleagues and I track the juncos throughout the day. We usually go from 7 a.m. through lunchtime. Then, after I take a break, I go back out until sunset. We hope to catch a lot of birds as the day goes on.

We measure them. We take preening oil samples by touching the preen gland with cotton swabs. We then store the swabs in individual tubes. In the evening, we label the tubes and write reports of the work we did. It's a long day, but rewarding when we get many samples."[4]

Whittaker sends the preen oil samples to other scientists who analyze the chemicals in the oil. They discovered that both male and female juncos have the same seventeen smelly compounds.[5] However, male juncos have more of some of the compounds, while females have more of others. This makes males and females smell different.[6]

"To me, juncos have a subtle smell. They smell like plants, probably like those that are in the same forest they live," said Whittaker.

Whittaker took samples of preen oil throughout the seasons. She discovered that the birds smell different as the seasons change.[7]

"In the winter, they produce very small amounts of these seventeen compounds. The amounts go up dramatically during the summer breeding season," said Whittaker. "This clue suggested that juncos could be using their perfume when choosing a mate."[8]

Next, Whittaker was curious about how juncos produce their scent.

An Unexpected Discovery

One day, Whittaker gave a talk about her work with the juncos to a small group of scientists. One of the attendees was Kevin

Theis, a researcher who studies how microbes help mammals communicate with smells.

"When I gave my talk, Theis recognized the names of the seventeen chemicals in the junco's preen oil. He said, 'Those are microbial compounds. Have you ever thought about looking at the bacteria in the preening gland?'" Soon after that, Theis and Whittaker started working together.[9]

Kevin Theis holds a hyena that has been anesthetized, or put to sleep temporarily, to take samples and measurements.

Prior to Whittaker and Theis, other scientists had discovered that the bacteria living in the preening gland makes compounds that kill a type of bacteria that damages the junco's feathers. However, nobody had looked at the bacteria as perfume makers.

"It intrigued me greatly that nobody had explored the role of microbes in junco's scent," said Theis. "We work as a team. Whittaker goes to the field, catches the juncos, takes samples of preen oil, and sends them to me in small tubes. In my lab, I do experiments to find out the types of bacteria present in the preen oil samples."[10]

Theis is a microbial ecologist. He studies the microbiome, the communities of microbes that live on or inside animals. Before working with juncos, Theis had discovered that bacteria make the hyenas' "perfume."[11] He was now curious to see whether bacteria did the same for juncos.

When Theis studied the samples of preen oil, he discovered many bacteria. Most of these bacteria can produce the airborne chemicals found in the preen oil. Although Theis and other scientists already knew that bacteria can make perfume for mammals, it was a first for birds.

Working together, Whittaker and Theis have solved the secret of the junco's perfume. They are the first scientists to discover that juncos do not make their own perfume by themselves. Bacteria in the preen oil make most of the junco's scent, and juncos seem to use this perfume to find mates.

WHAT IS THE MICROBIOME?

"I tell my ten-year-old daughter that she, like every other living organism, has billions of microbes living with her on her body. Most of these microbes do not make her sick; on the contrary, they help her stay healthy. For instance, they help her digest food she cannot digest on her own or fight microbes that do cause disease," said Theis.[12] The microbiome is a natural part of our body. Scientists are studying how the microbiome and the organisms they live in work together. Maybe one day the microbiome will help us prevent or fight diseases.

3
THE MYSTERY OF MAMA BEAR

First thing in the morning, Sam Steyaert sits at his desk in the offices of the Scandinavian Brown Bear Research Project in Tackåsen, Sweden. He downloads the Global Positioning System (GPS) data from the night before into his computer. He leans back, sips his coffee, and waits for the data to appear on the screen.

The GPS data comes from collars attached to the Scandinavian brown bears. Throughout the day, the GPS devices record the location of bears in the area. Steyaert is particularly interested in where the bears have been all night when they are most active.

Brown bears, such as this one pictured in a Scandinavian forest, are active during spring and early summer, when they look for mates.

As the computer analyzes the GPS data, it marks dots on a map on the screen. The computer connects the dots. Steyaert now knows where each bear has been. On the screen, Steyaert puts together the paths of several bears. He can now see which bears crossed ways and which stayed apart. During late summer and fall, males and females cross paths often. They remain in the same area to feed, getting ready for winter. But now, Steyaert is looking at the data from spring and early summer. He pauses. The data looks different.[1]

Between the mating season from early May and mid-July, some mama bears with cubs do not cross paths with males. They do not eat, sleep, or travel in the same zone where males roam. This pattern repeats every season. What could that mean?

What Male Bears Do

It's a male bear thing. During the mating season, males can be very aggressive toward cubs that are not theirs. Steyaert has found that males kill about three of every ten cubs. Mama bears do what they can to protect their cubs. Sometimes they try to defend them.

> **Science Tongue Twister:**
> **The scientific name of the Scandinavian brown bear is *Ursus arctos*, Latin for "brown bear."**

But males are larger and stronger than females. After the mating season ends, the cubs are no longer victims of male bear attacks.

Looking at the GPS data has given Steyaert an idea. During the mating season, when the cubs are in danger, mama bears move away from the males. Sometimes the food in these areas is not as abundant and rich as it is where the males are; nevertheless, they remain in these areas, and the mama bears eat less.[2]

Once the mating season is over and the cubs are no longer in danger of male attacks, mama bears and cubs return to areas where males are. Mama bears now feast on better foods. Steyaert thinks that mama bears might have developed a strategy to protect their cubs from angry males.[3] Now he needs to prove that the "move-away" tactic can really save cubs' lives.

Steyaert and Boss, Bear Crime Scene Investigators

Steyaert needed to play detective to test his idea. Would moving away from areas with males protect the cubs from male bear attacks? During the mating season, Steyaert tracked males and females again with the GPS data. He found that some

A mama bear with two cubs watches for dangerous male bears.

BEAR FACTS

- **The brown bear is one of the largest carnivores on land, head-to-head with the polar bear.**

- **The largest brown bears live in Kamchatka, Russia, and Katmai, Alaska.[9] These brown bears can grow as tall as a professional soccer goal (2.4 meters or 8 feet) and as heavy as ten golden retriever male dogs (a total of 320 kilograms or 700 pounds). Nevertheless, they can run fast and react swiftly.**

- **All grizzly bears are brown bears, but not all brown bears are grizzly bears.**

mama bears with cubs moved to an area in which they did not cross paths with males. He also found other mama bears with cubs that remained in areas where males lived.[4]

Every morning, Steyaert studied the GPS data collected on the night before. He found out whether any mama bears had crossed paths with males. Then he went out into the forest to see with his own eyes what happened when the males and mama bears came close to each other.

Steyaert went to the forest with Boss, his bear-tracking dog. Boss is a Jämthund, a type of dog typically trained for moose and bear hunting. Boss looks a lot like a wolf with a curly tail. He helps Steyaert find bear tracks, scat, and sometimes the actual bears.[5]

Guided by the GPS maps, Steyaert and Boss tracked bears.

When they found the area where males and mama bears had crossed paths, they tried to figure out what happened. Had there been a fight? What had happened to the cubs?

The detective work paid off. After analyzing many crime scenes with Boss, Steyaert confirmed his idea. Mama bears that stay out of the way of males kept more cubs alive than mama bears that had crossed paths with males.[6]

Still, Steyaert was curious. Bears can travel long distances; they could have easily entered the mama bears' territories. What kept the males from going where the females had moved?

The Enemy of My Enemy Is My Friend

Steyaert looked closely at the GPS maps. He studied the areas where mama bears preferred to live with their cubs during mating season. He then looked at where males lived. What was the difference?

A bear cub is sleeping in a den, safe from danger.

Steyaert soon realized that mama bears had chosen areas of the forest that were close to people's homes. However, these areas were not so close that people would become concerned about having a bear almost in their backyard.[7] Males, Steyaert knew, try to stay as far away from people as possible. For bears, man is the top predator.

Steyaert discovered that mama bears have learned that being relatively close to people can be to their cubs' advantage. By living in areas that males avoid because they are too close to people, mama bears keep males away from their cubs. This "human shield" keeps bear cubs alive until mating season is over.[8]

4
PIG GRUNTS TELL A STORY

Veterinary doctor Marianne Wondrak steps into the open field of the Haidlhof Research Station in Vienna, Austria, and whistles. The long whistle alerts the pigs that it's time to eat. Every day at noon, Wondrak serves their food—vegetable scrapings mixed with barley and wheat—in a trough located in their usual feeding spot.[1] Maxime García, a biologist who studies how animals communicate, has teamed up with Wondrak to try to figure out what pig grunts mean. He's been working with this group of pigs for several months, but still looks forward to see-ing the pigs' response to Wondrak's lunch call.

"The pigs have learned that Wondrak's whistle means feeding time. When they hear it, all forty of them rush toward the food. They scream and grunt loudly. It is impossible to know which animal produces which sound," said García. "One would think that they haven't eaten in weeks. They were just feeding on grass when Wondrak whistled. It's always fun to watch!"[2]

Kunekune pigs run toward the researcher in response to a lunch call.

García and Wondrak work with short-legged, stocky kunekune pigs. These pigs are very sociable, friendly, and kind among themselves and with people. "They grunt and squeal loudly, constantly to each other," said García. "Other scientists and I think that pigs use these sounds to communicate with each other. We think that they pass on information about themselves and their environment."[3]

For animals that live in groups as pigs do, it is important to communicate with each other. Animals need to tell males and females apart. Parents need to be able to recognize their own young and their young to recognize them. Males would benefit from knowing the size of other males challenging them. Scientists think that sound is one way that pigs can convey this information.

Before working with kunekune pigs, García had worked with boars. Boars are wild relatives of domestic pigs. They also grunt and squeal constantly. "We tend to underestimate boars and pigs," said García. "They communicate in very complex ways, which are still a mystery to us. I wanted to unravel part of that mystery."[4]

Marianne Wondrak pets a kunekune pig.

From Boars to Kunekune Pigs

Working with boars in the wild was nothing like working with kunekune pigs. "The boars were not used to having people around them," said García. "Getting close to them to get good sound recordings was a real problem. I had to stay up all night and part of the day for a few weeks to get as much good data as possible."[5]

On the other hand, it was not a problem at all to get close to the kunekune pigs. The pigs are free to roam in the open fields of the research station, but they are in contact with people from the day they are born. They are tame and friendly. Wondrak is in charge of the pig research station.[6]

"One of the things I do at Haidlhof Research Station is to train the pigs to enter a small experimental house for various studies. García makes sound recordings in these huts," said Wondrak.[76]

Kunekune pigs spend time outdoors even during winter, when they dig under the snow looking for food.

"For me, working with the pigs in the field is the best part of my work," said García.

García wanted to know whether pig grunts have cues about the animal's size. Pigs grunt with their vocal tract. The vocal tract includes the upper throat, the mouth, and the nose. The sound of grunts deepens when the vocal tract grows.

García wanted to know whether the pig's vocal tract grows as the entire body grows. If this were true, then pig grunts would deepen as the pig's body grew. The grunts would then be cues to the size of the pig's body.[8]

Maxime García recorded pig grunts in these huts.

Grunt Recordings and Pig X-rays

Early in the morning, Wondrak whistles and the pigs grazing in the pasture run toward her. It will be a busy day. García and others in the team will weigh the pigs, take X-rays of their vocal tracts, and record their grunts. Then García will analyze the data.

> **Science Tongue Twister: The scientific name of the kunekune pig is *Sus scrofa domesticus*.**

Squealing and grunting, the pigs surround Wondrak. She offers food treats and rubs their bellies to keep them distracted. Then, García calls one of the pigs by name. He offers food to convince the pig to follow him.

"I led the piglet to a small hut to record its grunts. The piglet was used to sleeping or finding shelter in this hut. It would not be stressed out during the recordings," said García. "The hut also allowed me to keep other pigs out. The thick wood walls and stacks of hay inside the hut cut down the background noise. This helped me make better recordings."[9]

Sometimes, García recorded pig grunts in the open field.

García waited a few seconds before offering food to the piglet. "The pig grunted repeatedly and I recorded it with my microphone," said García.

Later in the day, García and Wondrak measured the piglet's vocal tract with a portable X-ray machine.

A FRIENDLY WELCOME

The kunekune pigs are a free-range breed that is originally from New Zealand.[12] Adult pigs and piglets are indeed very playful. When you visit the Haidlhof Research Station for the first time, kunekune pigs will come to you grunting, asking for a belly rub only a few minutes after they meet you!

Researcher Marianne Wondrak hugs a kunekune pig after a day of working together in the field.

"We created a small sling with towels and jean pants. We made small holes to let the pig's legs through," said García. "The piglets were not anesthetized; they were not put to sleep temporarily. They were most often calm for a couple of minutes, which was enough. We took X-rays from their neck and heads. I weighed them. After that, we led the pigs back to grazing."[10]

What Pigs Say

After many months of collection, García analyzed the data with his computer. He was delighted to have confirmed his hypothesis. As the piglets grew into adults, their vocal tracts also grew and the grunts became deeper. Pig grunts contain reliable cues about the pig's size.[11] García would now like to know whether pigs could understand these cues and use them to know other pigs better.

5
ALLIGATOR BELLOWS

As a teenager, crocodile biologist Stephan Reber volunteered at the Zurich Zoo in Switzerland. He answered questions about reptiles, showed live snakes to visitors, and even let people touch some of the reptiles.

"Zurich's was the first zoo in Europe to breed critically endangered Siamese crocodiles," said Reber. "We observed things that were new. Even the keepers who had been working with crocodiles for years were amazed. The crocodile father became more and more interested in his babies. It patiently

34

waited until the mother let him get close to them," said Reber. "After a few weeks, the entire family was lying together under the heat lamp; the little ones were climbing onto their father's back. This was new to us because all the books claimed that male crocodiles would kill and eat baby crocs. All of this made me realize how little we know about crocodiles." Reber was hooked.[1]

To nobody's surprise, Reber studied biology at the University of Zurich. Later, he studied animal behavior as a doctorate student in the University of Vienna in Austria. He was studying how ravens communicate, but was not completely happy with this topic alone. His doctorate advisor saw

Stephan Reber introduces zoo visitors to Hunter, an American alligator. Do not attempt to do what Reber does in this photo. He has much experience around alligators.

this and said to Reber, "As long as you finish your main project, you can do an additional project on whatever you want, on any species you want ... even on alligators!"

"Although, my advisor probably intended to make a joke with his last remark, I instantly knew that was what I wanted to do!" said Reber.[2]

What Crocs Say

Crocodilians are a large group of animals that includes crocodiles, alligators, caimans, and gharials. Crocodilians use their voices often. Both males and females bellow loudly when they interact with each other. They bellow more during the mating season. What are they saying? Nobody knows.

Many other animals also use their voices over long distances. Think for instance of owl hoots, monkey roars, and deer groans. Scientists think that some of these sounds contain clues about the animal's size. Scientists call these clues "formants" because the vocal tract "forms" the sounds.[3]

A female Chinese alligator in the wild bellows often to other alligators.

For a deer, knowing the size of another deer approaching is important because size matters when it comes to defending territory. Formants in deer groans vary with the size of the animal. The bigger the deer, the deeper the formants are. Scientists think that deer can communicate their size to other deer with formants. However, nobody had studied whether alligators could do the same.

Reber had found what he wanted to study in alligators, but alligators are not easy to work with. He needed to find the right alligator and the best way to record its bellows.

From Vienna, Austria, to Florida, USA

With the help of his advisor's connections in Florida, Reber spent several months at the St. Augustine Alligator Farm Zoological Park. The park has a lagoon with forty-three American alligators, which are up to about 13 feet (4 meters) long. It would not be easy to put any of these alligators in a chamber to record its bellows.

One day, as Reber was walking by a large cube-shaped container he heard alligator bellows coming from the inside. The zookeepers had placed a single 4-foot (1-meter) Chinese alligator inside the container to recover from an illness. The alligator could move easily inside the container, which had enough room to fit a large washing machine. Reber had a Eureka moment! "She's small," he thought of the alligator. "And I can turn this container into an air-tight, waterproof chamber!"[4]

Stephan Reber holds the Chinese alligator he worked with during the experiments. Note that tape is keeping the alligator's snout closed.

With the help of one of the zoo engineers, Reber modified the container. He waited until the alligator recovered from her illness to begin his study.

A Chinese Alligator in Heliox

To study whether alligator bellows have formants, Reber used a method that had worked repeatedly in other animals. He recorded alligator bellows when the animal was breathing regular air. He then compared those recordings with those made when the alligator was breathing a mixture of helium and oxygen, also known as "heliox."[5]

Helium is an inert gas that does not cause harm. However, breathing heliox changes the formants in an animal's voice, making them sound higher. This also happens to people when they inhale helium from a balloon. If alligator bellows had formants, the bellows would sound higher when the animal breathed heliox.

How to Record Alligator Bellows

It is about 5:30 a.m., and Reber is heading toward Alligator Park. He retrieves the recording equipment from the main building next to the Komodo dragon enclosure. He then prepares the container for the Chinese alligator. He will first record bellows while the alligator is breathing regular air. With the alligator inside the container, Reber fills it about halfway with water. He covers the tank with a plastic tarp and seals it tight. He waits a few minutes to let the alligator get used to the surroundings. The alligator can raise its head above the water to breathe or remain below the water for a few minutes.[6]

To make the alligator bellow, Reber played back the alligator's own sounds that he had recorded beforehand. Every time Reber played the recording, the alligator raised her head above the water, tilted it back, and bellowed. Reber recorded the bellows with a microphone placed next to the container.

Next, Reber recorded the bellows when the alligator was breathing heliox. First, Reber replaced the air in the container with a mixture of helium and oxygen stored in gas tanks. He removed the air above the water by raising the water level in the container until it was very close to the top. As the water level rose, it pushed the air out of the container through a tube on the side. Then,

WHY HELIUM CHANGES SOUND

Sound traveling in helium is higher because it goes faster than in regular air. The faster sound travels, the higher the frequency, hence the higher sound. Sound travels faster because helium is lighter than air. The same happens when sound travels in heliox, a mixture of helium and oxygen.

Reber checks on the Chinese alligator submerged in the experimental tank.

Reber added heliox to the container while he lowered the water level to about half. The alligator remained submerged during the few minutes it took Reber to change the air for heliox.[7]

This setup was used to record alligator bellows. The alligator is inside the tightly sealed, white container in the middle. The black box to the left is the speaker. To the right is the microphone on a tripod.

After waiting several minutes to let the alligator get used to these changes, Reber played back the call again. This time he paid close attention to the bellows. If the bellows changed in heliox, then Reber would know right away that alligator bellows had formants.

Science Tongue Twisters:
The scientific name of the Chinese alligator is *Alligator sinensis*. The American alligator's scientific name is *Alligator mississippiensis*.

The alligator raised her head above the water, tilted it back, and bellowed. Reber smiled. The bellows in heliox sounded clearly different from those in normal air. Reber confirmed the result when he analyzed the bellows with his computer.[8] The secret is out! Alligator bellows have formants that might tell other alligators information about their size.

HANDS-ON ACTIVITY

Sound Effects

Many animals use their vocal chamber to make a variety of sounds. The vocal cords make the original vibrations that produce the sounds. These sound waves travel through the vocal chamber, which may change and then alter the original sound. For example, deer can make their vocal chamber longer, which makes the sounds it produces deeper. Scientists think that animals can use some of these different sounds to communicate with each other.

In this experiment, you will change the length of a "vocal chamber" using hollow tubes of different sizes and hear how the length of the tube affects the sound produced when you strike the tubes with a straw.

What you need:
★ 4 drinking straws (#1–4 in figure)
★ 4 hollow tubes, such as those used for holding flowers up (transparent tubes #6–9 in figure)
★ 1 hard straw, such as those used in drinking cups with a lid (#5, center of figure)

What to do:
1. Cut straws #2–4 and hollow tubes #7–9 to the lengths indicated in the table.
2. Assemble straw #1 by inserting one straw inside another and then cutting one end to the size indicated on the table.
3. Repeat step 2 with the hollow tubes.
4. Hold straw #1 with one hand and strike the upper half several

times with the striped straw.

5. Repeat with straws #2–4. Listen to the sounds.

6. Repeat steps 4–5 with the transparent hollow tubes.

Results:

- Were the sounds the same or different after striking the straws or tubes of different lengths?
- How can you explain this result?

Explore further:

Using a pan flute, produce the same sustained sound through the different pipes of the flute.

Can you make a musical instrument with the straws and hollow tubes of the experiment?

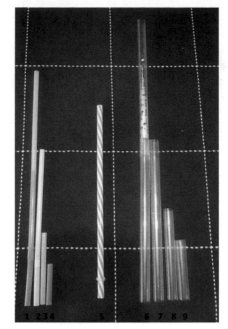

Cut the straws and hollow tubes as shown in this image.

SIZES OF STRAWS AND HOLLOW TUBES ON FIGURE									
Length (approx.)	1	2	3	4	5	6	7	8	9
centimeters	29	18	8	4	22	35	18	10	6
inches	11	7	3	2	9	14	7	4	3

★ CHAPTER NOTES ★

CHAPTER 1: The Secret of the Smart Bird's Brain

1. Dr. Pavel Němec, Skype interview with author, September 26, 2016.
2. Ibid.
3. Kevin J. McGowan, "Frequently Asked Questions about Crows," Cornell Lab of Ornithology, http://www.birds.cornell.edu/crows/crowfaq.htm#raven (accessed November 26, 2016).
4. Seweryn Olkowicz, M. Kocourek, R. K. Lučan, M. Porteš, W. T. Fitch, S. Herculano-Houzel, and P. Němec, "Birds Have Primate-Like Numbers of Neurons in Their Forebrain," *Proceedings of the National Academy of Sciences* 113 (2016): 7255.
5. Ibid.
6. Ibid.

CHAPTER 2: The Secret of the Junco's Perfume

1. Dr. Danielle Whittaker, phone interview with author, September 1, 2016.
2. Ibid.
3. Danielle Whittaker and Kevin Theis, "Bacterial Communities Associated with Junco Preen Glands: Preliminary Ramifications for Chemical Signaling," Chapter 8 in A. B. Schulte, et al., eds., *Chemical Signals in Vertebrates*, (Switzerland: Springer International Publishing, 2016), p. 105.
4. Dr. Whittaker.
5. Danielle Whittaker, K. M. Richmond, A. K. Miller, R. Kiley, C. Bergeon Burns, J. W. Atwell, and E. D. Ketterson, "Intraspecific Preen Oil Odor Preferences in Dark-Eyed Juncos (*Junco hyemalis*)," *Behavioral Ecology* 22 (2011): 1256.
6. Danielle Whittaker, H. A. Soini, N. M. Gerlach, A. L. Posto, M. V. Novotny, and E. D. Ketterson, "Role of Testosterone in

Stimulating Seasonal Changes in a Potential Avian Chemosignal," *Journal of Chemical Ecology* 37 (2011): 1349.

7. Whittaker and Theis.

8. Danielle Whittaker, N. M. Gerlach, H. A. Soini, M. V. Novotny, and E. D. Ketterson, "Bird Odour Predicts Reproductive Success," *Animal Behaviour* 86 (2013): 697.

9. Dr. Kevin Theis, phone interview with author, August 24, 2016.

10. Dr. Whittaker.

11. Kevin Theis, A. Venkataraman, J. A. Dycus, K. D. Koonter, E. N. Schmitt-Matzen, A. P. Wagner, K. E. Holekamp, and T. M. Schmidt, "Symbiotic Bacteria Appear to Mediate Hyena Social Odors," *Proceedings of the National Academy of Sciences USA* 110 (2013): 19832.

12. Dr. Theis.

13. Dr. Whittaker.

CHAPTER 3: The Mystery of Mama Bear

1. Dr. Sam Steyaert, Skype interview with author, October 11, 2016.

2. S. M. J. G. Steyaert, M. Leclerc, F. Pelletier, J. Kindberg, S. Brunberg, J. E. Swenson, and A. Zedrosser, "Human Shields Mediate Sexual Conflict in a Top Predator," *Proceedings of the Royal Society B* 283 (2016), doi 10.1098/rspb.2016.0906.

3. Dr. Stayaert.

4. Stayaert, et al.

5. Dr. Stayaert.

6. Stayaert, et al.

7. Ibid.

8. Ibid.

9. Dr. Stayaert.

CHAPTER 4: Pig Grunts Tell a Story

1. Dr. Marianne Wondrak, Skype interview with author, October 20, 2016.

2. Dr. Maxime García, Skype interview with author, September 20, 2016.

3. Ibid.

4. Ibid.

5. Ibid.

6. Haidlhof Research Station, University of Veterinary Medicine in Vienna, Austria, https://www.vetmeduni.ac.at/en/messerli/science/cognition/research-station-haidlhof/> (accessed November 12, 2016).

7. Dr. Wondrak.

8. Maxime García, M. Wondrak, L. Huber, and T. Fitch, "Honest Signaling in Domestic Piglets (*Sus scrofa domesticus*): Vocal Allometry and the Information Content of Grunt Calls," *Journal of Experimental Biology* 219 (2016): 1913.

9. Dr. García.

10. Ibid.

11. García, et al.

12. Haidlhof Research Station.

CHAPTER 5: Alligator Bellows

1. Dr. Stephan Reber, Skype interview with author, September 19, 2016.

2. Ibid.

3. Stephan A. Reber, T. Nishimura, J. Janisch, M. Robertson, and W. T. Fitch. "A Chinese Alligator in Heliox: Formant Frequencies in a Crocodilian," *Journal of Experimental Biology* 218 (2015): 2442.

4. Dr. Reber.

5. Reber, et al.

6. Ibid.

7. Ibid.

8. Dr. Reber.

★ GLOSSARY ★

boar ★ A wild pig.

breeding season ★ Season of the year in which animals mate to have babies; also called mating season.

chemical ★ Any substance made of matter.

endangered ★ Living organism that is at a serious risk of extinction.

forebrain ★ The frontal part of the brain.

formant ★ Sounds formed in the vocal tract of animals.

GPS ★ Global Positioning System; network of satellites that sends information used to calculate the position of objects on Earth.

heliox ★ A mixture of the gases helium and oxygen.

mammal ★ A warm-blooded animal that has hair, secretes milk to feed the young, and usually gives birth to live babies.

microbe ★ Organisms, such as bacteria, that are so small they can only be seen with a microscope.

microbiome ★ A group of microbes that live in a particular environment, such as the human body.

neuron ★ A cell of the nervous system that transmits nerve impulses; also called nerve cell.

predator ★ An animal that kills other animals.

preen ★ The act of birds cleaning and straightening their feathers with their beaks.

species ★ A group of similar living organisms that can have babies.

tame ★ An animal that is not dangerous to or frightened of people.

X-rays ★ Radiation used to take pictures of the inside of a body.

★ FURTHER READING ★

Books

Herbert Howell, Catherine. *Ultimate Explorer Field Guide: Reptiles and Amphibians: Find Adventure! Go Outside! Have Fun! Be a Backyard Ranger and Amphibian Adventurer.* Des Moines, IA: National Geographic Children's Books, 2016.

Riggs, Kate. *Amazing Animals: Brown Bears.* Mankato, MN: Creative Paperbacks, 2015.

Spinner, Stephanie. *Alex the Parrot: No Ordinary Bird: A True Story.* New York, NY: Knopf Books, 2012.

Turner, Pamela. *Crow Smarts: Inside the Brain of the World's Brightest Bird.* New York, NY: HMH Books for Young Readers, 2016.

Websites

National Geographic Kids

kids.nationalgeographic.com/animals/pig/#pig-fence.jpg

Read some cool facts about pigs.

PBS

pbs.org/video/1778560467/

Learn about Alex the parrot and Dr. Irene Pepperberg, the scientist who worked with him for thirty years.

★ INDEX ★